W9-BYX-365

My Guide to the
CONSTITUTION

THE
POWER OF
THE STATES

Tammy Gagne

Mitchell Lane
PUBLISHERS
P.O. Box 196
Hockessin, Delaware 19707

My Guide to the
CONSTITUTION

The Bill of Rights
The Executive Branch
The Judicial Branch
The Legislative Branch
The Power of the States
The Story of the Constitution

Copyright © 2012 by Mitchell Lane Publishers

All rights reserved. No part of this book
may be reproduced without written permission
from the publisher. Printed and bound in the
United States of America.

PUBLISHER'S NOTE: The Constitution of the
United States appears in the appendix to
My Guide to the Constitution: *The Story of
the Constitution*. The amendments to the
Constitution, including the Bill of Rights, appear
in My Guide to the Constitution: *The Bill of
Rights*.

The facts on which the story in this book
is based have been thoroughly researched.
Documentation of such research can be
found on page 44. While every possible effort
has been made to ensure accuracy, the
publisher will not assume liability for damages
caused by inaccuracies in the data, and
makes no warranty on the accuracy of the
information contained herein.

Printing   1   2   3   4   5   6   7   8   9

**Library of Congress
Cataloging-in-Publication Data**
Gagne, Tammy.
    The power of the states / by Tammy Gagne.
        p. cm.—(My guide to the Constitution)
    Includes bibliographical references and index.
    ISBN 978-1-58415-945-2 (library bound)
    1. States' rights (American politics)—Juvenile
literature. 2. Federal government—United
States—Juvenile literature. I. Title.
    JK311.G34 2011
    320.473'049—dc22
                                                    2011000613

Paperback ISBN: 9781612281872

eBook ISBN: 9781612280899

                                                    PLB

CONTENTS

Words in **bold** type can be found in the glossary.

Chapter 1
We the People

The Constitution of the United States is one of the country's oldest and most valuable documents. Virtually every right that U.S. citizens have comes from the Constitution. It is considered the highest law in the land.

The Constitution was written by a group of men called the framers. This group included George Washington, the man who would become the country's first president. It also included another highly esteemed person in U.S. history—Benjamin Franklin. The framers met at Independence Hall in Philadelphia, Pennsylvania, during the summer of 1787. This historic event is often referred to as the Constitutional Convention.

The framer given the most credit for the creation of the Constitution would become the country's fourth president, James Madison. In later years he was even called the Father of the Constitution because he was responsible for so much of the writing in the document. Madison was modest about the nickname, though. He insisted that the Constitution

Independence Hall

James Madison, 1805,
by Gilbert Stuart

was not "the offspring of a single brain," but "the work of many heads and many hands."

Every state except Rhode Island sent **delegates** to help create the Constitution. The leaders of Rhode Island worried that a strong national government would interfere with their own policies. Together the framers decided exactly what the document would state. This wasn't an easy task. Not everyone agreed on what the document should say, but they worked together nonetheless. When they finished, 39 of the 55 men signed it.

Before the Constitution could become a legal document, a certain number of states needed to **ratify** it. On December 7, 1787, Delaware became the first state to do this. Several other states followed soon thereafter, but others were more hesitant. They feared that the Constitution would not do enough to protect the freedoms of the people.

Not surprisingly, Rhode Island was the last state to ratify the Constitution. In 1788, the state held a popular election to ratify the document. The result was 237 votes in favor and 2,945 opposed. Rhode Island's approval did not come until May 29, 1790. Since signatures were needed from only nine states, the document was officially ratified when New Hampshire approved the document on June 21, 1788.

People who supported the Constitution as it was originally written were known as Federalists. The Federalists and their opponents, known as the Antifederalists, developed into our country's first political parties. The Federalists believed in a strong government, but the Antifederalists worried that too much power would be given to the president or Congress. The Antifederalists included Samuel Adams, Patrick Henry, and George Mason.

Again, Madison played a key role. With the help of Alexander Hamilton and John Jay, Madison wrote *The Federalist Papers*. This series of 85 essays explained the intent of the Constitution. Madison and his coauthors hoped the information would convince the citizens of New York to ratify the Constitution. *The Federalist Papers* are considered a vital part of U.S. history. The essays were first published in New York newspapers anonymously. In fact, the authors' names were not revealed until 1818, when the essays were first published in a bound collection.

New York finally ratified the Constitution in the summer of 1788, but two other states were still unconvinced. Fortunately, the framers designed the Constitution so that lawmakers could add to it as needed. The first set of **amendments** to the Constitution was the Bill of Rights. The addition of these ten amendments finally convinced North Carolina and Rhode Island to ratify the Constitution two years after its creation.

The Bill of Rights

Amendment I

Congress shall make no law respecting an establishment of religion, or prohibiting the free exercise thereof; or abridging the freedom of speech, or of the press; or the right of the people peaceably to assemble, and to petition the Government for a redress of grievances.

Amendment II

A well regulated Militia, being necessary to the security of a free State, the right of the people to keep and bear Arms, shall not be infringed.

Amendment III

No Soldier shall, in time of peace be quartered in any house, without the consent of the Owner, nor in time of war, but in a manner to be prescribed by law.

Amendment IV

The right of the people to be secure in their persons, houses, papers, and effects, against unreasonable searches and seizures, shall not be violated, and no Warrants shall issue, but upon probable cause, supported by Oath or affirmation, and particularly describing the place to be searched, and the persons or things to be seized.

Amendment V

No person shall be held to answer for a capital, or otherwise infamous crime, unless on a presentment or indictment of a Grand Jury, except in cases arising in the land or naval forces, or in the Militia, when in actual service in time of War or public danger; nor shall any person be subject for the same offence to be twice put in jeopardy of life or limb; nor shall be compelled in any criminal case to be a witness against himself, nor be deprived of life, liberty, or property, without due process of law; nor shall private property be taken for public use, without just compensation.

Amendment VI

In all criminal prosecutions, the accused shall enjoy the right to a speedy and public trial, by an impartial jury of the State and district wherein the crime shall have been committed, which district shall have been previously ascertained by law, and to be informed of the nature and cause of the accusation; to be confronted with the witnesses against him; to have compulsory process for obtaining witnesses in his favor, and to have the Assistance of Counsel for his defence.

Amendment VII

In Suits at common law, where the value in controversy shall exceed twenty dollars, the right of trial by jury shall be preserved, and no fact tried by a jury shall be otherwise re-examined in any Court of the United States, than according to the rules of the common law.

Amendment VIII

Excessive bail shall not be required, nor excessive fines imposed, nor cruel and unusual punishments inflicted.

Proposed Bill of Rights

Congress of the United States,

begun and held at the City of New York, on Wednesday, the fourth of March, one thousand seven hundred and eighty nine.

The Conventions of a number of the States having, at the time of their adopting the Constitution, expressed a d... prevent misconstruction or abuse of its powers, that further declaratory and restrictive clauses should be added: And as extending the ground of pub... the Government, will best insure the beneficent ends of its institution:

Resolved, by the SENATE and HOUSE of REPRESENTATIVES of the UNITED STATES of AMERICA in C... two thirds of both Houses concurring, That the following Articles be proposed to the Legislatures of the several States, as Amendments to the Con... States; all, or any of which articles, when ratified by three fourths of the said Legislatures, to be valid to all intents and purposes, as part of the s...

Articles in addition to, and Amendment of the Constitution of the United States of America, proposed b...

by the Legislatures of the several States, pursuant to the fifth Article of the Original Constitution.

Article the first ...... After the first enumeration required by the first Article of the Constitution, there shall be one Representative for every th... number shall amount to one hundred, after which, the proportion shall be so regulated by Congress, that there shall be not less than two hundred R... Representatives, nor less than one Representative for every forty thousand persons, until the number of Representatives... hundred, after which, the proportion shall be so regulated by Congress, that there shall not be less than two hundred R... than one Representative for every fifty thousand persons. [Not Ratified] ... the compensation for the services of the Senators and Representatives, shall take effect, until an ele...

... of religion, or prohibiting the free exercise thereof; or abri... ... the Government for a redress of gr... ... keep and bear Arm...

Amendment IX

The enumeration in the Constitution, of certain rights, shall not be construed to deny or disparage others retained by the people.

Amendment X

The powers not delegated to the United States by the Constitution, nor prohibited by it to the States, are reserved to the States respectively, or to the people.

The First Amendment made it possible for people to disagree with the government. U.S. citizens have the right to speak their minds without the worry of being punished when other people do not share their opinions. The right to disagree is one of the most meaningful rights granted by the Constitution. This right has paved the way for many more positive changes to the Constitution. Each of its twenty-seven amendments was created when someone realized a need for further change.

The Constitution made it possible for the government to grow and change according to the needs of the nation, not according to the needs of the government. It divided responsibility among three separate branches—the executive branch (headed by the president), the legislative branch (headed by Congress), and the judicial branch (headed by the Supreme Court). The purpose of this design was to create checks and balances. No branch of government has more power than another. But where do the states fit into all this?

The Capitol Building

Today, more than 220 years after the ratification of the U.S. Constitution, people still disagree about how much power the states should keep. Instead of going to war with one another, however, the states look to the Constitution as a way of deciding what should be done. When the states cannot agree on an issue, the Supreme Court hears the case and makes a decision on the matter. The balance of power that the framers created continues to help the federal government run.

The framers also had the states in mind when they designed the Constitution. They wanted the states to keep a certain amount of power, and that power has been evident throughout the country's history. Every amendment to the Constitution has been the result of one or more states inciting change in one way or another.

The original U.S. Constitution is considered one of the country's most valuable documents. It is housed in Washington, D.C., at the National Archives, where visitors can view it. All four pages are displayed in a special glass case that regulates temperature and humidity to make sure it is still there for future generations.

When Each State Ratified the U.S. Constitution		
STATE	DATE	VOTE
Delaware	December 7, 1787	30-0
Pennsylvania	December 12, 1787	46-23
New Jersey	December 18, 1787	38-0
Georgia	January 2, 1788	26-0
Connecticut	January 9, 1788	128-40
Massachusetts	February 6, 1788	187-168
Maryland	April 28, 1788	63-11
South Carolina	May 23, 1788	149-73
New Hampshire	June 21, 1788	57-47
Virginia	June 25, 1788	89-79
New York	July 26, 1788	30-27
North Carolina	November 21, 1789	194-77
Rhode Island	May 29, 1790	34-32

Chapter 2
The Question of Power

Because the document had to be ratified by each state, the power of the states began with their approval of the Constitution. One might even argue that, with this requirement, the framers granted the states more power than the federal government. At the same time, the creation of the Constitution took a certain number of rights away from the states. Which rights remained with the states and which ones were withheld from them?

The 10th Amendment, the last of the Bill of Rights, addresses the rights of the states. It specifies that whatever powers the Constitution does not give to the federal government, or deny to the states, belong to the states or to individuals. Like many other parts of the Constitution, though, this single sentence has been interpreted several different ways over the last two centuries.

Not even Supreme Court justices have agreed on how to interpret the 10th Amendment. Chief Justice John Marshall, who served from 1801 to 1835, was

Statue of John Marshall, at
John Marshall Park in
Washington, D.C.

JOHN MARSHALL

CHIEF JUSTICE OF THE UNITED STATES
1801 — 1835

The Constitutional Convention was inspired by Shays' Rebellion, an uprising in Massachusetts. A monument to the event, named for Revolutionary War hero Daniel Shays, stands in Sheffield, Massachusetts.

known for giving higher consideration to the rights of the federal government than to those of the states. An 1819 Supreme Court case (*McCulloch v. Maryland*) provides an excellent example. Marshall and the rest of the court ruled that Congress had the right to set up a national bank in the state of Maryland. They also decided that Maryland did not have the right to tax the institution, since it had been established by the federal government according to the Constitution.

When Justice Marshall died in 1835, Roger Taney (TAW-nee) became the court's new chief justice (1836–1864). Taney's views were very different from Marshall's. He thought that dual sovereignty should exist. In other words, both the national government and the states could have powers that would not take away from each other's rights.

In the years that followed, attitudes of Supreme Court justices shifted several times. The Great Depression and World War II saw Supreme Court justices who focused more on national power. This view continued through the civil rights era of the 1960s. The 1970s and 1980s, however, brought a return to a greater balance of power between the federal government and the states.

Chief Justice William Rehnquist in particular was known for favoring the dual sovereignty mindset. A 1997 Supreme Court case (*Printz v. United States*) gives us an example. In this case the Supreme Court failed to uphold the Brady Handgun Violence Protection Act. This act of Congress required state and local law enforcement officers to perform background checks prior to approving the sale of a handgun. The court ruled that the law interfered with the states' rights of commerce in relation to the 10th Amendment.

The powers that the Constitution denied the states are a bit clearer. Most of these powers can be found within Article I, Section 10 of the document. Nearly all of them address the rights the Constitution gives exclusively to the federal government.

Article I

Section 10. No state shall enter into any Treaty, Alliance, or Confederation; grant Letters of Marque and Reprisal; coin Money; emit Bills of Credit; make any Thing but gold and silver Coin a Tender in Payment of Debts; pass any Bill of Attainder, ex post facto Law, or Law impairing the Obligation of Contracts, or grant any Title of Nobility.

No state shall, without the Consent of the Congress, lay any Imposts or Duties on Imports or Exports, except what may be absolutely necessary for executing its inspection Laws: and the Net Produce of all Duties and Imposts, laid by any State on Imports and Exports, shall be for the Use of the Treasury of the United States; and all such Laws shall be subject to the Revision and Controul [sic] of the Congress.

No State shall, without the Consent of Congress, lay any Duty of Tonnage, keep Troops, or Ships of War in time of Peace, enter into any Agreement or Compact with another State, or with a foreign Power, or engage in War, unless actually invaded, or in such imminent danger as will not admit of delay.

The Constitution clearly affirms that no state can become the ally of a foreign country on its own. During times of peace, states cannot keep warships or organize armies without the permission of the federal government. They also cannot join with other states or with foreign countries to wage war. They may, however, join forces in this way if they are invaded and federal troops cannot come to their aid in a reasonable amount of time.

States also are not allowed to make their own money. This too is the responsibility of the federal government.

The Constitution denies states the right to make any law that affects the past (these are called ex post facto laws). This means that people cannot be punished for acts that violated a law before the law existed. Along these same lines, no state law can change the terms of a contract that has already been drawn up and signed. The national government cannot do either of these things as well.

State laws cannot bestow titles of nobility to any person. They also cannot "pass any Bill of Attainder," which means make laws that single out a person or group for punishment without fair and proper court proceedings. Again, these are things the federal government cannot do, either.

The Constitution also removed the states' ability to charge a fee for items imported to or exported from their boundaries. If a state does charge this **unconstitutional** tax, the money received will become property of the United States Treasury.

Article IV addresses relationships between the states.

Article IV

Section 1. Full Faith and Credit shall be given in each State to the public Acts, Records, and judicial Proceedings of every other State. And the

Independence Hall in Philadelphia, painted by Ferdinand Richardt around 1860. Philadelphia was the U.S. capital from December 1790 until June 1800.

Congress may by general Laws prescribe the Manner in which such Acts, Records and Proceedings shall be proved, and the Effect thereof.

Section 2. The Citizens of each State shall be entitled to all Privileges and Immunities of Citizens in the several States.

A Person charged in any state with Treason, Felony, or other Crime, who shall flee from Justice, and be found in another State, shall on Demand of the executive Authority of the State from which he fled, be delivered up, to be removed to the State having Jurisdiction of the Crime.

Section 3. New states may be admitted by Congress into this Union; but no new State shall be formed or erected within the Jurisdiction of any other State; nor any State be formed by the Junction of two or more States, or Parts of States, without the Consent of the Legislatures of the States concerned as well as of the Congress.

The Congress shall have Power to dispose of and make all needful Rules and Regulations respecting the Territory or other Property belonging to the United States; and nothing in this Constitution shall be so construed as to Prejudice any Claims of the United States, or of any particular State.

Section 4. The United States shall guarantee to every State in this Union a Republican Form of Government, and shall protect each of them against Invasion; and on Application of the Legislature, or of the Executive (when the Legislature cannot be convened), against domestic Violence.

In this article, the Constitution limits state laws that might infringe upon the laws of other states. Each state must recognize other states' acts and records. For example, Florida and New Jersey have different laws pertaining to marriage, divorce, and adoption. To comply with the U.S. Constitution, Florida must acknowledge a legal marriage, divorce, or adoption performed in New Jersey.

Article IV also prevents states from discriminating against citizens of other states. States cannot prevent citizens from other states from owning property, for example. Certain privileges, however, can be granted to residents of the state—such as lower costs for a college education.

It denies states the right to hide other states' **fugitives**. A person cannot commit a crime in one state and run to another for protection. If a crime has been committed, the governor of the state where it took place can demand the return of the suspected criminal.

Congress has the right to admit new states to the Union. Individual states, however, cannot create a new state within their boundaries. They also cannot **secede**, or become a separate country or union.

According to Section 4 of Article IV, each state must be run as a **republic**—the people vote for representatives, including the governor, and these representatives vote or perform according to the will of their supporters. A state cannot put a dictator of any kind in place to make decisions. The power of the states actually comes from the power of the people who live in the states.

Similar to the U.S. Constitution, each individual state also has a constitution. A state constitution contains the highest laws for that state. This document, however, cannot surpass or override the U.S. Constitution. The purpose of a state constitution is to provide a blueprint for the way that state will be run by its leaders. To view your state's constitution, visit http://www. constitution.org/ cons/usstcons.htm.

Criminals learn that running to another state for protection is pointless.

Chapter 3
Changing Powers of the States

In many ways the U.S. Constitution was centuries ahead of its time. Although the framers could not have envisioned every issue that would arise, they allowed for them nonetheless. The right to amend the Constitution is one of the greatest the framers included for the country. Most of the amendments to the Constitution relate to issues that arose after the document's creation.

Amendment XI

The Judicial power of the United States shall not be construed to extend to any suit in law or equity, commenced or prosecuted against one of the United States by Citizens of another State, or by Citizens or Subjects of any Foreign State.

One of the biggest disputes involving the states' rights concerns **sovereign immunity**, or the government's protection against being charged with a crime. As the states saw it, sovereign immunity

The Constitution

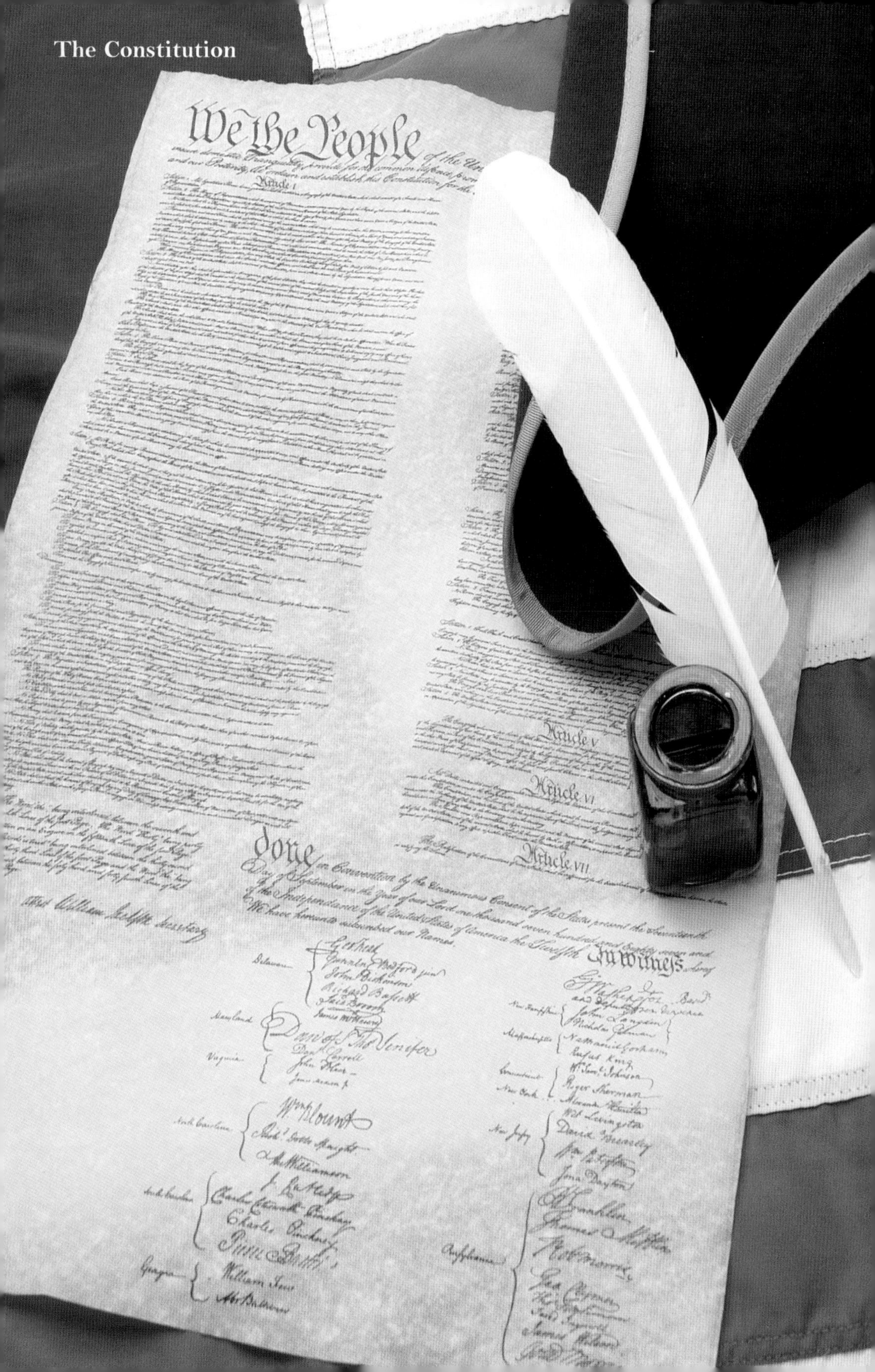

prevented a person from suing a state without the state's permission. Of course, common sense tells us that no state would give its permission to be sued. To complicate matters, not everyone interpreted this part of the Constitution the same way.

The problem reached the Supreme Court in 1793 with the case of *Chisholm v. Georgia.* Alexander Chisholm of South Carolina brought this lawsuit against the state of Georgia on the grounds of breach of contract. Chisholm was a merchant who had provided Georgia with clothing during the Revolutionary War. He claimed the state did not pay him for these goods. The state maintained that the Constitution protected it from the suit through its sovereign immunity.

United States Attorney General Edmund Randolph argued for Chisholm in the case *Chisholm v. Georgia.* Georgia insisted that the case was unconstitutional, since it was a "sovereign" state.

In a surprising decision, the Supreme Court found in favor of Chisholm. Just two days later a senator submitted a proposal to Congress to pass what is now the 11th Amendment. It affirms that no one who is not a citizen of the state can sue a state in federal court.

Ratified in 1795, the 11th Amendment did not put an end to disputes over sovereign immunity. Arguments about how to interpret the amendment continue to this day. When Congress passed the 14th and 15th Amendments, they forced the states to be responsible if they violated a person's rights through discrimination.

Some people still think that lawsuits against the states are unconstitutional. Others argue that removing the right to sue the states opens the door to discrimination.

The 11th Amendment also protects the states from lawsuits of a different kind. It prevents citizens of foreign countries from suing any of the states. This part of the amendment has caused far fewer debates.

ONE MAN'S TREASURE BECOMES THE GOVERNMENT'S LOOT?

In 1971, state officials from Florida tried to use the 11th Amendment to claim sunken treasure. The *Nuestra Señora de Atocha* sank 40 nautical miles from Key West in 1622. The ship was left undiscovered at the bottom of the ocean for more than 350 years. When Mel Fisher and his fellow treasure hunters found the wreckage, Florida tried to claim that the ship belonged to the state under Florida law. Florida insisted that the 11th Amendment protected the state from being sued for rightful ownership. In 1982, however, the U.S. Supreme Court finally ruled in favor of Fisher. The treasure was indeed his.

Chapter 4

The States' Power through History

In the nineteenth century, the disagreement about the division of power between the federal government and the states led to civil war. The northern states thought slavery should be outlawed throughout the country, but the southern states disagreed. They thought that each state should decide for itself whether to end slavery or not.

The southern states maintained that the federal government did not have the right to make this decision for them. When Abraham Lincoln was elected president in 1860, Congress worried that the Union was in jeopardy. Trying to prevent civil war, they passed a hurried amendment to protect slavery where it already existed. The change came too late, however. The southern states had already moved to secede from the Union, an act that violated the Constitution.

The Civil War began in 1861 at Fort Sumter in South Carolina. The northern states prevailed when the war ended in 1865. As a result, the 13th

A drawing of Franklin and Armfield, a slave-trading company in Alexandria, Virginia. The piece, called a broadside, was meant to raise awareness for the antislavery movement.

Confederate attack against Fort Sumter

Amendment was added to the Constitution. It proclaimed that slavery would no longer exist in any state in the Union. Few amendments have had such a profound effect on our nation's history.

Amendment XIII

Section 1. Neither slavery nor involuntary servitude, except as a punishment for crime whereof the party shall have been duly convicted, shall exist within the United States, or any place subject to their jurisdiction.

Section 2. Congress shall have power to enforce this article by appropriate legislation.

The 14th Amendment went a step further. Ratified in 1868, it granted citizenship, and all the rights that go along with it, to any person born in the United States and to any person granted U.S. citizenship. It removed the states' ability to take away a citizen's life, freedom, or belongings without proper cause under the law. This meant that all former slaves were now U.S. citizens and were entitled to the same rights as everyone else. (Native Americans were not given citizenship until 1924; they did not obtain full voting rights until the Voting Rights Act was renewed in 1975.)

Amendment XIV

Section 1. All persons born or naturalized in the United States, and subject to the jurisdiction thereof, are citizens of the United States and of the state wherein they reside. No state shall make or enforce any law which shall abridge the privileges or immunities of citizens of the United States; nor shall any state deprive any person of life, liberty, or property, without due process of law; nor deny to any person within its jurisdiction the equal protection of the laws.

Section 2. Representatives shall be apportioned among the several states according to their respective numbers, counting the whole number of persons in each state, excluding Indians not taxed. But when the right to vote at any election for the choice of electors for President and Vice President of the United States, Representatives in Congress, the Executive and Judicial officers of a State, or the members of the Legislature thereof, is denied to any of the male inhabitants of such State, being twenty-one years of age, and citizens of the United States, or in any way abridged, except for participation in rebellion, or other crime, the basis of representation therein shall be reduced in the proportion which the number of such male citizens shall bear to the whole number of male citizens twenty-one years of age in such State.

Section 3. No person shall be a Senator or Representative in Congress, or elector of President and Vice-President, or hold any office, civil or military, under the United States, or under any State, who, having previously taken an oath, as a member of Congress, or as an officer of the United States, or as a member of any state legislature, or as an executive or judicial officer of any state, to support the Constitution of the United States, shall have engaged in insurrection or rebellion against the same, or given aid or comfort to the enemies thereof. But Congress may by a vote of two-thirds of each House, remove such disability.

Section 4. The validity of the public debt of the United States, authorized by law, including debts incurred for payment of pensions and bounties for services in suppressing insurrection or rebellion, shall not be questioned. But neither the United States nor any State shall assume or pay any debt or obligation incurred in aid of insurrection or rebellion against the United States, or any claim for the loss or emancipation of any slave; but all such debts, obligations and claims shall be held illegal and void.

Section 5. The Congress shall have power to enforce, by appropriate legislation, the provisions of this article.

The 15th Amendment was the third change to the Constitution that resulted from the Civil War. Ratified in 1870, it prevented both federal and state governments from denying the right to vote based on a person's race or history as a slave. At this time only men had the right to vote.

Amendment XV
Section 1. The right of citizens of the United States to vote shall not be denied or abridged by the United States or by any state on account of race, color, or previous condition of servitude.

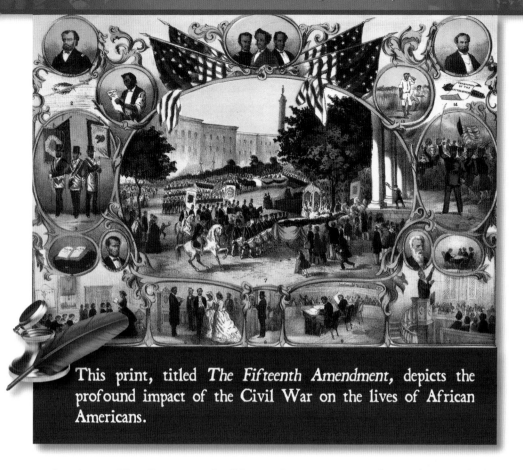

This print, titled *The Fifteenth Amendment,* depicts the profound impact of the Civil War on the lives of African Americans.

Section 2. The Congress shall have the power to enforce this article by appropriate legislation.

The war may have ended, but some battles raged on. Some southern states did everything they could to work around the 15th Amendment. They began charging poll taxes, which many newly freed slaves could not afford. They also passed literacy laws. This meant that a person had to know how to read in order to vote. Because so many freed slaves could not read, this effectively took away the voting rights that the 15th Amendment granted them.

The fight for civil rights continued through to the mid-twentieth century. Several southern states used **segregation** as a means of working around laws that called for equal rights for everyone. They insisted that African Americans were equal but separate. African

Americans could not attend the same schools, eat in the same restaurants, or ride in the same sections on a city bus as other people could.

The 1950s and '60s were a time of huge political change, caused by changing attitudes toward civil rights. People like Martin Luther King Jr. and Rosa Parks sparked the movement. These people spoke out about the injustices facing African Americans at this time. They helped many people realize that the issue of civil rights should matter to everyone.

It was the Supreme Court, though, that made true racial equality a reality under the law. On the 1954 case of *Brown v. Board of Education*, the Court ruled that segregation was not fair. Although it took a full decade to implement it, Congress passed an important piece of civil rights legislation. The Civil Rights Act of 1964 ended segregation in schools, in the workplace, and in public.

The women's **suffrage** movement also began at the state level. In this case it was the western states (then considered territories) that moved toward change for equality. While race no longer played a part in a person's right to vote, gender did. The women's rights movement began around the time the Civil War was brewing. It took many more years for equality to reach both sexes. Some even say that the battle still rages on.

In 1872, charges were filed against a woman named Susan B. Anthony for voting in that year's election. Anthony, an early women's rights activist, was prosecuted for the crime. Three years later the Supreme Court heard its first case on the issue (*Minor v. Happersett*). It unanimously rejected the argument that the 14th Amendment gave women the right to vote along with everyone else.

In 1878 a constitutional amendment was proposed that would prevent states from denying the right to vote based on gender. It was proposed again and again for the next 41 years. In 1890, the Territory of Wyoming officially became a U.S. state. Since the territory already allowed women the right to vote, it also became the first state to do so. Wyoming was joined by Utah, Colorado, and Idaho in providing this right over the following decade.

Susan B. Anthony was
arrested in 1872 for
trying to vote in a
presidential election.

A 1909 cartoon by E. W. Guston shows the fear that many men felt about the prospect of equal rights for women.

Suffrage parade, New York City, May 6, 1912

At the beginning of the twentieth century, suffrage for women had attracted many more supporters. Again, though, many southern states fought this growing change. In 1919 Congress finally had the two-thirds majority it needed to create a constitutional amendment granting women voting rights. The only thing standing in the way was ratification. Many people worried that the state of Tennessee would refuse to approve the amendment. A twenty-four-year-old senator named Harry Burn, however, surprised everyone by casting his vote in favor of the passage. The 19th Amendment was ratified in 1920.

Amendment XIX

The right of citizens of the United States to vote shall not be denied or abridged by the United States or by any state on account of sex.

Congress shall have power to enforce this article by appropriate legislation.

Not even these important changes ended debates about the states' rights and equality, however. Following the civil rights movement, people began to worry that **affirmative action** programs resulted in reverse discrimination. Many states set quotas for minorities and women in the workplace and in colleges as a way to ensure that race was not standing in the way of equal opportunity.

A 1978 Supreme Court case (*Regents of the University of California v. Bakke*) involved this issue. In this matter the Court ruled that denying a white student enrollment to medical school was unfair, since other students with lower tests scores were accepted on the basis of their race. The Court said that schools could not reserve spots for people based on their race. At the same time, the Court did concede that schools could consider race when making enrollment decisions.

A Bakke protest

Many people rallied for a more detailed constitutional amendment for equal rights during the 1970s. **Feminists** argued that women were not receiving the same level of pay and opportunity in the workplace as men were at this time. In 1972, Congress passed the Equal Rights Amendment. It specifically prevented discrimination on the basis of gender, but the states failed to ratify it. Opponents to the amendment thought it was unnecessary. They insisted that federal laws already provided equal rights for women.

FROM THE STATE OF CALIFORNIA TO THE SUPREME COURT

Although the Equal Rights Amendment did not pass, equality for women continued to move forward. One undeniable sign was the appointment of the country's first female Supreme Court justice in 1981. When Sandra Day O'Connor began her legal career, no private law firms would hire her. The only offer she received was for a legal secretary's position. She had better luck finding work with the state of California. There she became a deputy county attorney of San Mateo. After marrying, moving to Arizona, and starting a family, she continued her work in public service. She served as an assistant attorney general, a state senator, and a state judge before being appointed to the Supreme Court by President Ronald Reagan. She served on the Court for 24 years.

Sandra Day O'Connor

Chapter 5

Continuing State Struggles

The framers probably would have been proud that the U.S. Constitution they drew up in 1787 is still considered such an important document. Although they designed the Constitution to grow and change with the country, none of them could have imagined all the things that have occurred during the last two centuries. From medicine to transportation to space travel, all aspects of life in the United States depend on decisions based on the Constitution.

One thing that probably wouldn't have surprised them, though, is that the states continue to struggle with the federal government for power. Countless laws vary from state to state. Most of these differences cause few problems on a wide scale. Some, though, present major dilemmas for the Supreme Court.

In current times, one of the most debated issues involving the rights of the states is illegal immigration. In 2010, the state of Arizona passed a highly controversial law in relation to this problem. The new law, called SB 1070, states that police officers have

All that separates the towns of Nogales, Arizona, and Nogales, Mexico, is a concrete-and-steel fence. It is guarded by U.S. Border Patrol agents, who try to prevent illegal crossings. Despite the agents' presence, the number of illegal crossings is high, and violence is common. The area is considered one of the most dangerous along the U.S.-Mexico border.

In May 2010, people gathered to protest against SB 1070 in front of Governor Jan Brewer's office in Arizona.

the power to stop and verify the immigration status of any person they suspect of being in the U.S. illegally.

Many Americans think this law is unconstitutional. They argue that the states are not allowed to create immigration laws. They see immigration as part of foreign affairs, an area of the law that is denied to the states. They are also worried that the law would lead to **racial profiling**. Still, Arizona isn't the only state that has created immigration laws. In 2010 alone, more than 200 state laws concerning this issue were put into place. Some Americans see Arizona's law as a matter of law enforcement, not legislation. The matter may have to be decided by the Supreme Court.

Many people on both sides of the issue think that widespread dissent was exactly what the state of Arizona had in mind when its legislature passed the law. Could Arizona have been sending a message to the federal government? The problem of illegal immigration has been growing by leaps and bounds in recent years. If the federal government denies the state the right to make laws about it, then the federal government will have to make a greater effort to resolve the issues surrounding it. If this is the case, consider the power just a single state has in influencing the Union.

Another issue causing major disagreement between the federal government and the states is health care. Both the executive and legislative branches of the government began working on a national

An uninsured protestor left her mark in front of a Blue Cross health insurance company office in San Francisco, California, in 2009.

President Barack Obama applauds the passage of the health care bill in 2010.

health care system in 2008. In 2010, President Obama signed legislation that would make it mandatory for every U.S. citizen to purchase health insurance.

Does the federal government have the right to tell people what to buy? Some people say yes. They think the Constitution covers the issue as a matter of interstate commerce. Others say no. They believe that forcing citizens to purchase health insurance goes beyond any law that Congress has passed in relation to commerce. Some people even think that mandatory health care violates the Constitution. Several states have already filed lawsuits over the matter. Like Arizona's immigration law, the universal health care law will likely come before the Supreme Court.

Another major struggle between the states and the federal government involves civil unions and gay marriage. Some states have passed laws making it possible for people of the same gender to marry. This issue has caused a great deal of heated debate at both the state and federal level. Remember, the Constitution requires states to recognize the marriage records of other states. Many **liberal** Americans think that every couple consisting of two adults should have the right to get married. Many **conservative** Americans, however, believe that marriage should be limited to couples of opposite sex.

Some politicians want to add an amendment to the Constitution that would define marriage as being between a man and a woman. One proposed amendment said, "Marriage in the United States shall consist only of the union of a man and a woman. Neither this Constitution, nor the constitution of any State, shall be construed to require that marriage or the legal incidents thereof be conferred upon any union other than the union of a man and a woman." In 2006, this Marriage Protection Amendment failed to pass in the U.S. Senate. The vote was 49 in favor to 48 opposed, but a two-thirds majority was necessary.

When asked about the issue, many politicians said they do not support gay marriage, but a fair number thought it would be wrong to create a constitutional amendment that limits a person's rights. All previous amendments dealing with individuals have granted rights, not taken them away. The only thing that is certain is that debates over this issue—and many others between the federal government and the states—are far from over.

In 2005, U.S. Representative Diana DeGette of Colorado spoke out against a proposed amendment to ban gay marriage.

FOR MY FRIENDS
EQUAL RIGHTS

In 2008, actress and comedienne Whoopi Goldberg exercised her constitutional right to protest California's Proposition 8.

Wherever you stand on the issues that concern the states and the federal government, you have as much say as every other U.S. citizen. The rights granted to you by the Constitution's First Amendment make it possible for you to speak your mind freely. Regardless of your race or gender, as a U.S. citizen, you will also have the right to vote for political candidates of your choice at both the state and national level once you are eighteen years old. The same Constitution that gives your state its rights also provides you with individual rights.

CAPITAL PUNISHMENT

One of the most controversial issues between the states and the federal government during the last century has been capital punishment, or the death penalty. In 1976, the Supreme Court heard cases (together known as *Gregg v. Georgia*) regarding the death penalty. It ruled that the death penalty was indeed constitutional. This ruling upheld many state death penalty laws. In 2005 (in *Roper v. Simmons*), however, the Court ruled that the death penalty could not be used for juvenile offenders (defined as people under eighteen years of age). At the time, the ruling prevented 72 young people on death row from being executed.

BOOKS

Hennessey, Jonathan. *The United States Constitution: A Graphic Adaptation.* New York: Hill and Wang, 2008.

Ransom, Candice F. *Who Wrote the U.S. Constitution? And Other Questions About the Constitutional Convention of 1787.* Minneapolis, Minnesota: Lerner Classroom, 2010.

Shelton, Paula Young. *Child of the Civil Rights Movement.* New York: Schwartz & Wade, 2009.

Travis, Cathy. *Constitution: Translated for Kids.* Austin, Texas: Synergy Books, 2006.

WORKS CONSULTED

American Civil Liberties Union, Voting Rights Act Timeline
http://www.aclu.org/voting-rights/voting-rights-act-timeline

Archibold, Randal C. "Arizona Enacts Stringent Law on Immigration." *The New York Times,* April 23, 2010. http://www.nytimes.com/2010/04/24/us/politics/24immig.html

The Constitution of the United States
http://www.archives.gov/exhibits/charters/constitution_transcript.html

Farber, Daniel A. *Retained by the People: The "Silent" Ninth Amendment and the Constitutional Rights Americans Don't Know They Have.* New York: Basic Books, 2007.

The Federalist Papers: Primary Documents of American History; Library of Congress
http://www.loc.gov/rr/program/bib/ourdocs/federalist.html

Illinois Institute of Technology; Chicago-Kent College of Law. *The Oyez Project:* U.S. Supreme Court Media. http://www.oyez.org/

Monk, Linda R. *The Words We Live By: Your Annotated Guide to the Constitution.* New York: Hyperion, 2003.

Murray, Shailagh. "Gay Marriage Amendment Fails in Senate." *Washington Post,* June 8, 2006.
http://www.washingtonpost.com/wp-dyn/content/article/2006/06/07/AR2006060700830.html

The National Coalition to Abolish the Death Penalty: *Roper v. Simmons*
http://www.democracyinaction.org/dia/organizations/ncadp/
pressRelease.jsp?key=48&t=

Ritchie, Donald A. *Our Constitution.* New York: Oxford University Press,
2006.

ON THE INTERNET

The Charters of Freedom: Declaration of Independence, The
Constitution, The Bill of Rights
http://www.archives.gov/exhibits/charters/

The Constitution
http://www.whitehouse.gov/our-government/the-constitution

Lloyd, Gordon. *Timeline of the Ratification of the Constitution.*
http://teachingamericanhistory.org/ratification/timeline-state.html

The White House: The Presidents
http://www.whitehouse.gov/about/presidents/

affirmative action (uh-FIR-muh-tiv AK-shun)—An effort to improve education and job opportunities for minorities and women.

amendment (uh-MEND-munt)—An official addition or change to a document.

conservative (kun-SUR-vuh-tiv)—A person who prefers traditional values and limited change.

delegate (DEL-ih-git)—A person sent to represent a group of people on official business.

feminist (FEH-mih-nist)—A person who believes in and works toward gender equality.

fugitive (FYOO-jih-tiv)—Someone who is running from the law.

liberal (LIH-buh-rul)—A person who believes in progress and reform.

racial profiling (RAY-shul PROH-fy-ling)—Judging people based on their race or racial characteristics instead of on their actions.

ratify (RAT-ih-fy)—To confirm by official approval.

republic (ree-PUB-lik)—A form of government in which the people vote for representatives, who cast their votes in a final decision.

secede (seh-SEED)—To withdraw from a union or alliance.

segregation (seh-grih-GAY-shun)—The act of separating.

sovereign immunity (SOV-rin ih-MYOO-nih-tee)—The government's protection against being charged with a crime or sued by the people.

suffrage (SUF-rij)—The right to vote.

unconstitutional (un-kon-stih-TOO-shuh-nul)—Counter to the laws outlined in the Constitution.

ABOUT THE AUTHOR

Tammy Gagne is the author of numerous books for adults and children, including *Ways To Help Chronically Ill Children* and *What It's Like to Be / Qué se siente al ser Sonia Sotomayor* for Mitchell Lane Publishers. She considers the U.S. Constitution to be one of the most important documents ever written. Viewing the Constitution in person at the National Archives in Washington, D.C., is among her most treasured memories. She resides in northern New England with her husband and son. One of her favorite pastimes is visiting schools to speak to kids about the writing process.